What Lincoln Said

W h a t Lin

To Graham, who knows more
about presidents than anyone
else I know
—S.L.T.

To Phoebe Yeh
—J.E.R.

Collins is an imprint of HarperCollins Publishers.
What Lincoln Said Text copyright © 2009 by Sarah L. Thomson Illustrations copyright © 2009 by James E. Ransome
Manufactured in China. All rights reserved. No part of this book may be used or reproduced in any manner whatsoever with-
out written permission except in the case of brief quotations embodied in critical articles and reviews. For information address
HarperCollins Children's Books, a division of HarperCollins Publishers, 1350 Avenue of the Americas, New York, NY
10019.   www.harpercollinschildrens.com   Library of Congress Cataloging-in-Publication Data is available.
ISBN 978-0-06-084819-4 (trade bdg.) — ISBN 978-0-06-084820-0 (lib. bdg.) Designed by Stephanie Bart-Horvath
1 2 3 4 5 6 7 8 9 10 ❖ First Edition

coln Said

By Sarah L. Thomson
Art by James E. Ransome

Collins
An Imprint of HarperCollinsPublishers

"The world seemed wider and fairer before me."
That was how Abraham Lincoln remembered the day he earned
his first dollar. A farm boy, Abe could plant and harvest, catch fish
in the creek, split rails for fences. And he could build a boat.

One summer he ferried passengers up and down a river. Two men hired Abe to row them out to their steamboat. Abe thought they might pay him a quarter. Then each tossed him a silver half dollar.

"I could scarcely believe my eyes," he said. "By honest work I had earned a dollar."

What else could he do if he tried?

When he grew up, Abe left his father's farm. He worked on a riverboat, clerked in a store, marched as a soldier (but never fought a battle). And he sat under trees, reading books on law. He planned to make a new life for himself, and studying law was the start.

When Lincoln rode into the town of Springfield, everything he owned fit in two saddlebags. He didn't know a single person there. "I am quite as lonesome here as I ever was in my life," he complained.

But six months later he was working as a lawyer. Nobody called him Abe anymore. They called him Lincoln or Mr. Lincoln.

When people were accused of crimes or needed to settle arguments, Lincoln presented their cases to a judge. Nobody worked harder than he did. "Leave nothing for tomorrow that can be done today," he advised. "Resolve to be honest at all events."

With a scar on his face and big ears that stuck out, Lincoln didn't win cases on his looks. He was so tall and skinny he seemed like a skeleton in clothes. But he knew how to make people laugh.

When someone called him "two-faced," he shot back, "If I had another face, do you think I would wear this one?"

Arguing about laws in court wasn't enough for Lincoln. He became a politician so he could *make* laws. His wife, Mary, encouraged him. She believed he could even be president. The idea made Lincoln laugh. "Just think of such a one as me as president!" he roared. But maybe Mary knew something her husband didn't.

In Lincoln's time, there were about four million slaves in the United States. Slaves were human beings treated like animals: forced to work, bought and sold, chained, beaten.

"If slavery is not wrong, nothing is wrong," Lincoln said. He ran for president after all, promising to keep slavery out of new states in the American West.

Lincoln won the election. After his victory, several Southern states decided to break away from the country. They wanted to make a new nation where slavery would always be legal. They said they weren't part of the United States anymore and didn't have to obey its laws—or its president.

Lincoln said the Southern states didn't have the right to leave. The United States was one country, and he would keep it that way.

But he hoped to do it without fighting. "We are not enemies, but friends," he said in his first speech as president. "We must not be enemies."

Lincoln couldn't stop the Civil War from breaking out. He hated the thought of soldiers killing and dying. "I cannot bear it," he said. "The suffering, the loss of life, is dreadful."

But he wouldn't back down. He was determined to keep the United States together.

After two years of fighting, Lincoln made a decision. He would sign the Emancipation Proclamation on New Year's Day. In the states that were fighting to break away from the country, slaves would be "forever free."

On January 1, 1863, Lincoln shook hands until his arm ached. He worried that his fingers might tremble as he signed his name. He didn't want anyone in years to come to look at the paper and think that he had hesitated.

Taking a moment to steady his hand, he wrote his name firmly and clearly.

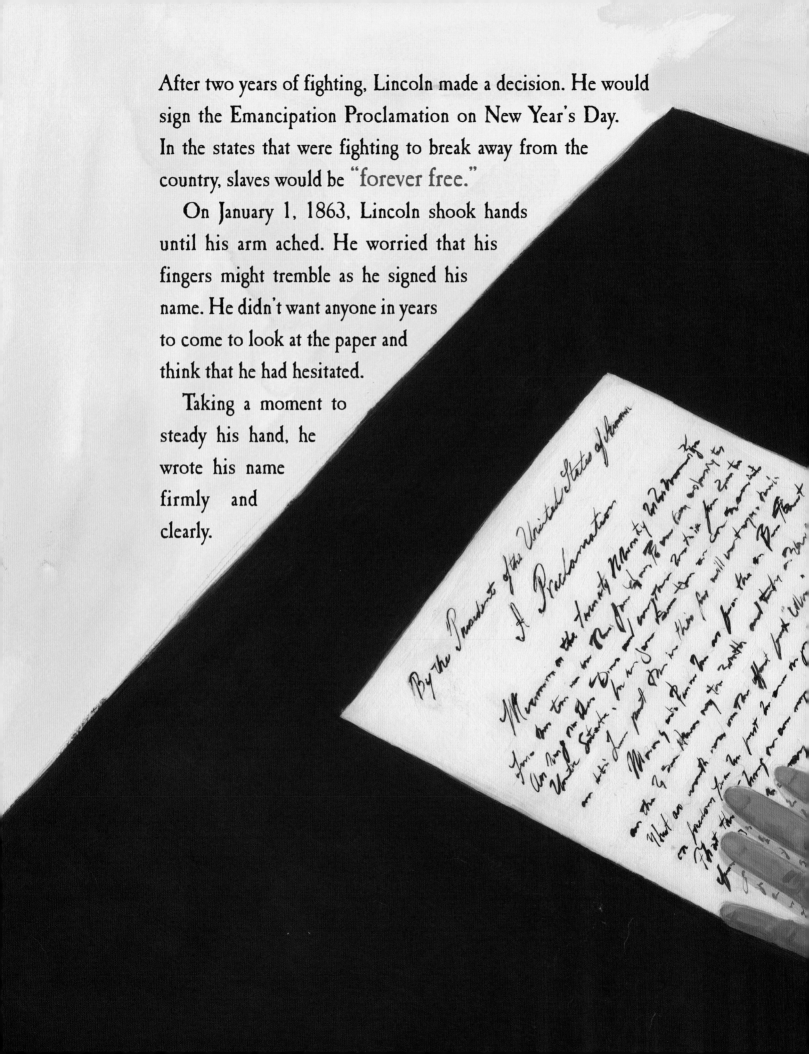

Lincoln knew one thing: Nothing else that happened in the war, nothing else that happened while he was president, would be as important as this moment. "If ever my name goes into history, it will be for this act," he said, "and my whole soul is in it."

Abraham Lincoln and Slavery

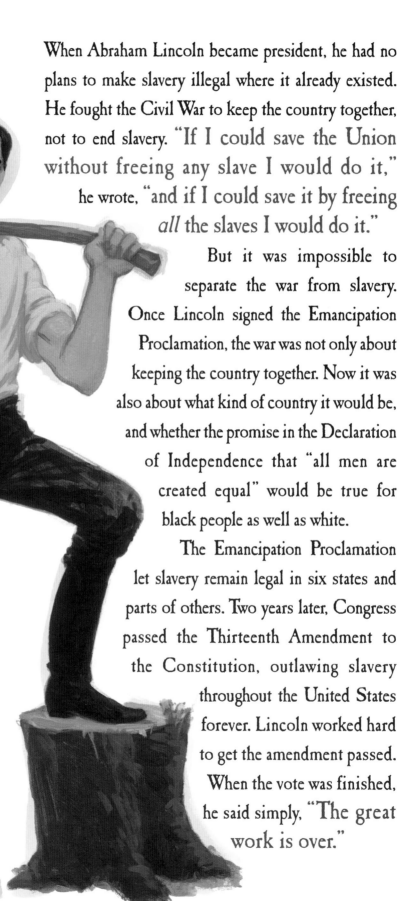

When Abraham Lincoln became president, he had no plans to make slavery illegal where it already existed. He fought the Civil War to keep the country together, not to end slavery. "If I could save the Union without freeing any slave I would do it," he wrote, "and if I could save it by freeing *all* the slaves I would do it."

But it was impossible to separate the war from slavery. Once Lincoln signed the Emancipation Proclamation, the war was not only about keeping the country together. Now it was also about what kind of country it would be, and whether the promise in the Declaration of Independence that "all men are created equal" would be true for black people as well as white.

The Emancipation Proclamation let slavery remain legal in six states and parts of others. Two years later, Congress passed the Thirteenth Amendment to the Constitution, outlawing slavery throughout the United States forever. Lincoln worked hard to get the amendment passed. When the vote was finished, he said simply, "The great work is over."

Timeline

1809	Lincoln is born in Kentucky.
1816	Lincoln's family moves to Indiana. He is 7 years old.
1818	Lincoln's mother dies when he is 9.
1819	Lincoln's father marries again. Lincoln's new stepmother is Sarah Bush Johnston.
1830	Lincoln's family moves to Illinois.
1831	Lincoln leaves home at 21. He settles in New Salem, Illinois, a town of about 100 people.
1834	Lincoln is elected to the state legislature to vote on laws for Illinois.
1837	Lincoln moves to Springfield, Illinois, and begins working as a lawyer.
1842	Lincoln marries Mary Todd, who is from a wealthy, slave-owning Kentucky family.
1843	Lincoln's son Robert is born.
1846	Lincoln's son Eddie is born.
1847	Lincoln is elected to the House of Representatives in Washington, D.C.
1850	Eddie dies at 3. Later that year, Lincoln's son Willie is born.
1853	Lincoln's son Tad is born.
1855	Lincoln runs for the U.S. Senate and loses.
1858	Lincoln runs for the U.S. Senate and loses again.
1860	Lincoln is elected president.
1861	The Civil War begins.
1862	Willie dies at 11. Lincoln signs the first Emancipation Proclamation.
1863	Lincoln gives the Gettysburg Address, dedicating a cemetery for soldiers.
1864	Lincoln is reelected as president.
1865	The Thirteenth Amendment, outlawing slavery, is passed. The Civil War ends. Lincoln is shot and killed by John Wilkes Booth while watching a play.

Author's Note

It's easy to admire Abraham Lincoln—for his eloquence, his shrewd intelligence, his ability to laugh at himself. But as I was doing the research for this book, I found myself most impressed by two contradictory traits—his flexibility and his strength of will. Throughout his life, Lincoln's ideas on slavery evolved. He listened to others and considered their views; the great speaker, writer, and abolitionist Frederick Douglass was one of those who influenced him. Lincoln was willing to change his mind. But when he had finally decided that, as president, he had the right and the moral authority to issue the Emancipation Proclamation, he would not back down from it, just as he would not back down from his best efforts to keep the Union together.

Illustrator's Note

When my editor, Phoebe Yeh, submitted Sarah's manuscript for *What Lincoln Said*, I realized on the first reading that I'd have to approach it in a manner I'd never done before. This book was humorous and lighthearted yet highly moving for me as an African American, especially when I reached the climax of the story when Lincoln signed the Emancipation Proclamation. So I didn't use live models for the artwork, which I usually do. Through numerous sketches in my sketchbook, I worked on developing how I wanted to paint Abe Lincoln. I really enjoyed the freedom to make any and everything possible, because the artwork wasn't limited by what a model could or could not do. For example, some body parts are elongated or exaggerated to elaborate the text.

In recent history, we have discovered that Lincoln was a very complex person, with many different sides that sometimes contradicted one another. However, I found it an honor and truly an indication of how far we've come in this country that an African American was, from my understanding, the first choice as an illustrator for this manuscript. In addition to this honor, Phoebe Yeh gave me the latitude and artistic freedom to depart from my usual style of illustration. In response to this trust, I am dedicating this book to her honor.